W9-CPW-058

Spending Money

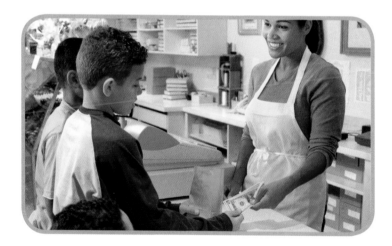

By Dana Meachen Rau

Reading consultant: Susan Nations, M.Ed., author/literacy coach/consultant

Gareth Stevens
Publishing

Please visit our Web site www.garethstevens.com. For a free color catalog of all our high-quality books, call toll free 1-800-542-2595 or fax 1-877-542-2596.

Library of Congress Cataloging-in-Publication Data

Rau, Dana Meachen, 1971–
    Spending money / by Dana Meachen Rau.
        p. cm. — (Money and banks)
    Includes bibliographical references and index.
    ISBN: 978-1-4339-3389-9 (lib. bdg.)
    ISBN: 978-1-4339-3390-5 (softcover)
    ISBN: 978-1-4339-3391-2 (6-pack)
————1. Money—Juvenile literature.   2. Consumption (Economics)—Juvenile literature.
    3. Finance, Personal—Juvenile literature.   I. Title.   II. Series.
    HG221.5.R38   2005
    339.4'7'083—dc22   2005042214

New edition published 2010 by
Gareth Stevens Publishing
111 East 14th Street, Suite 349
New York, NY 10003

New text and images this edition copyright © 2010 Gareth Stevens Publishing

Original edition published 2006 by Weekly Reader® Books
An imprint of Gareth Stevens Publishing
Original edition text and images copyright © 2006 Gareth Stevens Publishing

Art direction: Haley Harasymiw, Tammy West
Page layout: Daniel Hosek, Dave Kowalski
Editorial direction: Kerri O'Donnell, Barbara Kiely Miller

Photo credits: Cover, title page © White Packert/Iconica/Getty Images; pp. 4, 6, 8, 10, 16, 17, 19, 20 (upper right), 21 Shutterstock.com; pp. 7, 9, 12, 15, 18, Gregg Andersen; pp. 5, 11, 20 (left and lower right) Diane Laska-Swanke.

Printed in the United States of America

CPSIA compliance information: Batch #WW10GS: For further information contact Gareth Stevens, New York, New York at 1-800-542-2595.

Table of Contents

Boldface words appear in the glossary.

So Much to Buy!

Have you ever been to a shopping mall? Each store sells something different. You might pass a bookstore or a store that sells clothes. You might see a place to buy snacks or a shoe store. **Goods** and **services** are names for the two types of things you can buy with money.

Sometimes, deciding how to spend your money can be hard.

Goods are things you can buy and take home with you. Games, toys, and books are goods. The clothes you wear and food you eat are also goods. Can you think of other goods that you buy?

Apples from the grocery store are goods.

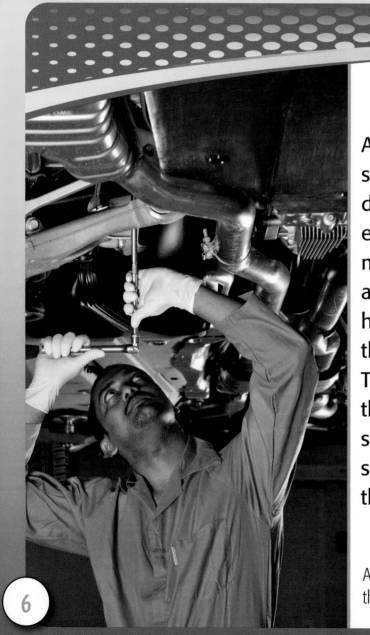

A service is something a person does for someone else. When a mechanic fixes another person's car, he or she is doing that person a service. The **customer** pays the mechanic for the service. What other services can you think of?

A mechanic performs a service that helps a car work properly.

Money Travels

Money travels when people spend it on goods and services. Let's say your mother gives you a dollar. You keep it in your piggy bank for a week. Then you might give the dollar to someone else to buy a book or a new toy. Money moving from person to person is called **circulation**.

When you buy a cookie at a bake sale, the money you spend moves to someone else.

The government makes coins and paper money. Coins are made of metal. They can last for many years. Paper money only lasts about a year and a half. Why do you think this is?

Coins are made at the United States Mint.

The government sends the money it makes to banks. The banks keep the money in locked safes called vaults. Guards at banks keep the money safe. They make sure the money will be there when customers need it.

Money travels to banks in trucks that keep the money safe.

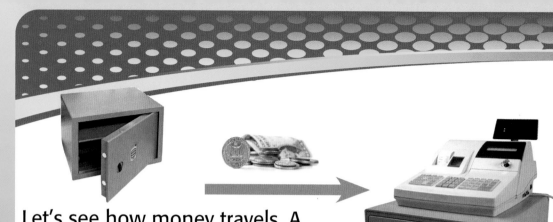

Let's see how money travels. A store owner goes to the bank to get money for her store.

Later that day, a man might buy a sandwich from her. The store owner gives the man **change**.

On his way home, the man might spend this change on a bottle of water. Money really gets around!

How Do I Pay?

Coins and paper money are called cash. You have probably used cash to buy things. Buying things with cash is easy, but using cash is not the only way to spend money.

Money is made in many different amounts. How many amounts do you see here?

Many people save their money in **accounts** at banks. They do not have to go to the bank every time they need to pay for something. They can use **checks** instead. Your aunt might send you a check on your birthday as a gift.

A check is a safe way to send money through the mail.

A check is a special slip of paper. It has places for your aunt to write your name, the date, and how much money she wants to give you. You can take the check to the bank and trade it for cash. The bank takes the money from your aunt's bank account.

A check must have your name written on it before you can trade it for cash.

Adults might pay for things with a **credit card**. A credit card is a small plastic card that fits in a **wallet**. A customer in a store can pay with a credit card instead of cash. Then the customer gets a bill in the mail to pay later. If the customer does not pay on time, they may have to pay the credit card company extra money.

A credit card has an account number on it. Each person's card has a different number.

Let's Make a Budget!

Let's say you have ten dollars to spend at a fair. What would you spend it on? You might be hungry and spend all of your money on snacks. Then you would not have any money left to play a game or to go on a ride.

Would you spend your money on a big pretzel or a ride on the merry-go-round?

15

You can plan how you will spend your money. This plan is called a **budget**. A budget can help you buy the goods and services you need. It can also help you know how much money you will have left over to buy things you want.

To plan a budget, you have to think carefully about how to spend your money.

Adults need to spend money on a home, food, and clothes. They pay for heat, electricity, and other things their homes need. They also save some of their money. Then they can plan for things they want. A family might spend money on a new TV. Adults also need to save money for unplanned events. For example, their car might break down and need to be fixed.

Going on a vacation is a fun way to spend money.

You can make a budget to decide how to spend your ten dollars before you go to the fair. You might plan to spend two dollars on food. You might plan to spend one dollar on games. You might plan to spend five dollars on rides. You might plan to spend one dollar on a balloon.

You can use a notebook to make a budget. Your budget is your spending plan.

If you followed your budget, you would have one dollar left. You could use that dollar for something you did not plan for. Maybe you will want another hot dog. Maybe you will want to go on another ride. You will have enough money to buy what you want when you plan ahead with a budget.

Planning helps you have enough money for the fun things you want to do.

Math Connection: A Budget at the Zoo

You are going on a field trip to the zoo. You have $10.00 to spend. Look at the list of goods and services at the zoo. Plan how you will spend your money by making a budget. Write your budget plan on a separate sheet of paper.

Tickets

Ticket to get
into the zoo
$6.00

=

Pony
ride
$2.00

=

Snacks

 =

Soft drink $1.50

 =

Popcorn $1.00

Gift Shop

Zebra pencil   25¢

  =

Stuffed giraffe $2.50

Extras

Food to feed
the goats   50¢

 =

Glossary

account: the money kept by a person at a bank

budget: a plan for how money will be spent

change: the money returned when cash used to pay for an item is more than the item costs

checks: special slips of paper that can be traded for cash by the person whose name is written on the checks or that can be used to pay for something

circulation: the movement of something, such as money, from person to person or from place to place

credit card: a small card that lets customers buy something now and pay for it later

customer: a person who pay for goods and services

goods: things you can buy and take home with you

service: something that someone does for someone else

wallet: a small, flat case for carrying money or credit cards

For More Information

Books

Hill, Mary. *Spending and Saving*. New York: Children's Press, 2005.

Houghton, Gillian. *Goods and Services*. New York: The Rosen Publishing Group, Inc., 2009.

Rosinsky, Natalie. *Spending Money*. Mankato, MN: Compass Point Books, 2004.

Web Sites

Kids and Money
www.ext.nodak.edu/extnews/pipeline/d-parent.htm
A newsletter for kids with tips on spending wisely

Kids' Money Kids' Page
www.kidsmoney.org/kids.htm
Filled with ideas and links to all money matters for kids

Publisher's note to educators and parents: Our editors have carefully reviewed these Web sites to ensure that they are suitable for students. Many Web sites change frequently, however, and we cannot guarantee that a site's future contents will continue to meet our high standards of quality and educational value. Be advised that students should be closely supervised whenever they access the Internet.

Index

About the Author

Dana Meachen Rau is an author, editor, and illustrator. She has written more than one hundred books for children, including nonfiction, early readers, and historical fiction. She lives with her family in Burlington, Connecticut.